The Empowered Professional

Copyright © 2024 by Luchrisha Harrison

All rights reserved. No part of this book may be reproduced, stored in a retrieval system, or transmitted in any form or by any means—electronic, mechanical, photocopy, recording, or otherwise—without the prior written permission of the publisher, except in the case of brief quotations embodied in critical articles and reviews.

Published by Luchrisha Harrison

ISBN: 9798333449016

Printed in United States

First Edition

The Empowered Professional

Affirmations, Meditation, and Manifestation Techniques for Career Growth

The Empowered Professional

Affirmations, Meditation, and Manifestation Techniques for Career Growth

Luchrisha Harrison

Introduction

Welcome to your journey of self-discovery, empowerment, and career success! This guide is designed to help you harness the power of daily affirmations, meditation, and manifestation techniques to achieve your career goals. Whether you're just starting out, looking to advance, or making a career change, this guide will provide you with the tools and strategies to navigate your path with confidence and clarity.

The Power of Positive Thinking

Understanding Positive Thinking
- Positive thinking is more than just being happy or optimistic. It involves maintaining a constructive and hopeful attitude, expecting positive outcomes, and focusing on solutions rather than problems. It's about creating a mindset that supports growth and success.
- Research shows that positive thinking can improve overall well-being, enhance performance, and increase resilience in the face of challenges. By fostering a positive mindset, you open yourself up to new opportunities and possibilities.

Benefits of Positive Thinking
- **Increased Motivation**: When you believe in your potential, you are more likely to set ambitious goals and pursue them with vigor.
- **Enhanced Problem-Solving**: Positive thinkers approach problems with a solution-oriented mindset, leading to more creative and effective solutions.

- **Better Health**: Positive thinking is linked to lower stress levels, better
- cardiovascular health, and a stronger immune system.
- **Improved Relationships**: A positive attitude can enhance your interactions with others, leading to stronger professional and personal relationships.

By combining the power of positive thinking, daily affirmations, meditation, and manifestation, you can create a clear path towards your career success. This guide will provide you with the tools and strategies to harness these powerful practices, helping you achieve your career goals and realize your full potential. Welcome to your journey of success!

NOTES

Understanding Your Career Goals

Identifying Your Passion

Understanding what drives you and where your passions lie is essential for career satisfaction and success. Here are some steps to help you identify your passions:

Reflect on Your Interests:
- Think about the activities or subjects that excite you the most. What do you enjoy doing in your free time? What topics do you find yourself constantly reading about or discussing?
- Consider your hobbies and any side projects. These can offer clues about your true passions.

Assess Your Skills and Strengths:

- Make a list of your skills, both hard (technical) and soft (interpersonal). What are you naturally good at?
- Seek feedback from colleagues, friends, and family. They can often see strengths in you that you might overlook.

Identify Your Values:
- Think about what is important to you in a job. Is it creativity, helping others, financial stability, or work-life balance?
- Align your career choices with your core values to ensure long-term fulfillment.

Explore Career Options:
- Research different industries and roles that align with your interests, skills, and values.
- Consider informational interviews with professionals in fields you're interested in to gain insights into their daily work and career paths.

NOTES

Setting SMART Goals

Setting clear and achievable goals is crucial for career development. Use the SMART criteria to create effective goals:

Specific:
- Clearly define what you want to achieve. Avoid vague goals. Instead of saying, "I want to advance in my career," say, "I want to become a team leader in my department."

Measurable:
- Establish criteria for measuring your progress. How will you know when you've achieved your goal? For example, "I will complete a leadership training course and take on a small project to lead within six months."

Achievable:

- Ensure your goal is realistic and attainable. Consider the resources and time you have available. Is your goal within reach given your current situation?

Relevant:

- Your goal should align with your broader career objectives and values. Ask yourself, "Does this goal move me closer to where I want to be in my career?"

Time-bound:

- Set a deadline for your goal to create a sense of urgency and keep yourself motivated. For example, "I will achieve this goal by the end of the year."

NOTES

Visualize Your Idea Career

Visualization is a powerful tool that can help you stay focused and motivated. Follow these steps to visualize your ideal career:

Create a Clear Mental Image:
- o Close your eyes and imagine your ideal workday. Where are you working? What tasks are you doing? Who are you working with? How do you feel?
- o Be as detailed as possible. The clearer the image, the more effective the visualization will be.

Use Visualization Tools:
- o **Vision Boards:** Create a physical or digital board with images, quotes, and symbols that represent your career goals.
- o **Guided Imagery:** Listen to guided visualization recordings to help you imagine your success.

Practice Regularly:
- o Spend a few minutes each day visualizing your career goals. The more you practice, the stronger and

more impactful your visualizations will become.

Stay Positive and Believe:
- Maintain a positive mindset and believe in your ability to achieve your goals. Visualization works best when combined with a strong sense of self-belief and optimism.

By understanding your passions, setting SMART goals, and visualizing your ideal career, you lay a strong foundation for success and fulfillment in your professional journey.

NOTES

Daily Affirmations

What Are Affirmations?

Affirmations are positive statements that can help you challenge and overcome negative thoughts. When you repeat them often, and believe in them, you can start to make positive changes. Affirmations can:

Reprogram Your Mind:
- Shift your focus from negativity to positivity.
- Replace self-doubt with confidence and determination.

Enhance Your Mental Health:
- Reduce stress and anxiety.
- Improve overall emotional well-being.

Boost Your Confidence:
- Reinforce your belief in your abilities and potential.
- Encourage a growth mindset.

NOTES

How Affirmations Work

Affirmations work through repetition and belief. Here's how to make the most out of your affirmations:

Consistency:
- o Repeat your affirmations daily, preferably in the morning and before bed.

- Incorporate them into your routine, such as during your commute or while getting ready.

Emotion and Conviction:
- Say your affirmations with emotion and conviction. Believe in the words you are saying.
- Visualize yourself achieving what the affirmation describes.

Present Tense:
- Phrase your affirmations in the present tense, as if they are already happening. For example, "I am confident and successful in my career."

Personalization:
- Customize your affirmations to reflect your personal goals and desires.
- Make them specific to your career path and what you wish to achieve.

NOTES

List of Daily Affirmations

Here are some powerful affirmations you can use daily to enhance your career:

Confidence and Self-belief:
- "I am confident in my skills and abilities."
- "I believe in my potential and my capacity to succeed."

Motivation and Drive:
- "I am motivated and driven to achieve my career goals."
- "Every day, I am making progress towards my dreams."

Overcoming Challenges:
- "I am resilient and can overcome any challenge."
- "I learn and grow from every experience."

Success and Achievement:
- "I attract success and abundance into my life."
- "I am achieving my career goals with ease and grace."

Positive Work Environment:

- o "I work in a positive and supportive environment."
- o "I collaborate effectively with my colleagues."

Balance and Well-being:
- o "I maintain a healthy work-life balance."
- o "I prioritize my well-being and self-care."

NOTES

Examples of Customized Affirmations

Here are some examples of how you can personalize your affirmations based on specific career goals:

- **For Leadership Roles:**
    - "I am a strong and effective leader. My team respects and values my guidance."
- **For Career Advancement:**
    - "I am attracting new opportunities for growth and advancement in my career."
- **For Creative Professions:**
    - "I am constantly inspired, and my creativity flows effortlessly."

For Sales and Performance Goals:
- "I consistently exceed my sales targets and contribute to my company's success."

NOTES

Creating Your Own Affirmations

To create your own personalized affirmations, follow these steps:

- **Identify Your Goals:**
  - o Clearly define what you want to achieve in your career.
  - o Break down your goals into smaller, manageable steps.
- **Formulate Positive Statements:**
  - o Convert each goal into a positive affirmation. For example, if your goal is to improve your public speaking skills, your affirmation could be, "I am a confident and engaging public speaker."
- **Keep It Short and Specific:**
  - o Ensure your affirmations are concise and to the point. This makes them easier to remember and repeat.
- **Write Them Down:**

- Write your affirmations in a journal or on sticky notes placed around your workspace.

Review and Revise:

- Regularly review your affirmations and update them as your goals and circumstances evolve.

NOTES

Tips for Effective Affirmations

Be Positive:
- Avoid negative words. Focus on what you want to achieve, not what you want to avoid.

Stay Realistic:

- While it's important to aim high, ensure your affirmations are realistic and attainable.

Incorporate Emotions:
- Include how achieving your goal will make you feel. For example, "I am thrilled and grateful to be promoted to a managerial position."

Repeat and Believe:
- Consistency is key. The more you repeat your affirmations, the more ingrained they become in your subconscious.

By incorporating daily affirmations into your routine, you can build a positive mindset that supports your career aspirations and personal growth.

NOTES

Introduction to Meditation

Benefits of Meditation for Your Career

Meditation can significantly enhance your career by improving your mental clarity, emotional stability, and overall well-being. Here are some specific benefits:

Improved Focus and Concentration:
- Regular meditation trains your mind to stay focused on tasks and reduces distractions, leading to higher productivity and efficiency.

Enhanced Creativity and Problem-Solving Skills:
- Meditation encourages a state of relaxation and openness, allowing for more creative thinking and innovative solutions to challenges.

Stress Reduction:
- By promoting relaxation and reducing stress hormones, meditation helps you manage work-related stress and maintain a calm demeanor.

Better Decision-Making:
- Meditation enhances your ability to make thoughtful, clear-headed decisions by reducing emotional reactivity and increasing awareness.

Increased Emotional Intelligence:
- Regular practice improves your self-awareness, empathy, and ability to manage relationships effectively, which are crucial skills in any career.

NOTES

Types of Meditation

There are various forms of meditation, each with unique techniques and benefits. Here are some popular types that can support your career goals:

Mindfulness Meditation:
- o Focuses on being present in the moment and observing thoughts and sensations without judgment.
- o Benefits: Enhances focus, reduces stress, and improves emotional regulation.

Guided Meditation:
- o Involves listening to a guide who leads you through visualizations or relaxation exercises.
- o Benefits: Helps beginners get started, promotes deep relaxation, and can be tailored to specific goals like career success.

Transcendental Meditation:
- Involves silently repeating a mantra to achieve a state of deep relaxation and heightened awareness.
- Benefits: Reduces stress, improves concentration, and enhances overall well-being.

Loving-Kindness Meditation:
- Focuses on developing feelings of compassion and love towards oneself and others.
- Benefits: Increases empathy, reduces negative emotions, and fosters positive relationships.

Body Scan Meditation:
- Involves mentally scanning the body from head to toe, observing any sensations and releasing tension.
- Benefits: Enhances body awareness, reduces stress, and promotes relaxation.

NOTES

How to Get Started with Meditation

Starting a meditation practice can be simple and accessible to everyone. Here's how you can begin:

- **Choose a Comfortable Space**:
    - Find a quiet, comfortable space where you won't be disturbed. It could be a dedicated meditation room, a corner of your office, or a peaceful outdoor spot.
- **Set a Time**:
    - Decide on a time that works best for you, whether it's first thing in the morning, during a lunch break, or before bed. Consistency is key.
- **Start Small**:
    - Begin with just a few minutes each day and gradually increase the duration as you become more comfortable. Even five minutes of meditation can be beneficial.
- **Adopt a Comfortable Posture**:
    - Sit or lie down in a comfortable position. You can sit cross-legged on the floor, in a chair with your feet flat on the ground, or lie down on your back.

Focus on Your Breath:

- Close your eyes and take slow, deep breaths. Focus on the sensation of the breath entering and leaving your body. This helps anchor your mind and brings your attention to the present moment.

Use Guided Meditations:

- If you're new to meditation, consider using guided meditations available through apps, websites, or meditation classes. These can provide structure and support as you develop your practice.

Be Patient and Gentle with Yourself:

- It's normal for your mind to wander during meditation. When you notice this, gently bring your focus back to your breath or chosen point of focus. Over time, you'll find it easier to maintain concentration.

NOTES

Creating a Meditation Routine

Incorporating meditation into your daily routine can help you make it a consistent habit. Here are some tips:

Set an Intention:

- Begin each session by setting an intention or goal. This could be to reduce stress, improve focus, or cultivate gratitude.

Use Reminders:
- Set reminders on your phone or calendar to meditate at your chosen times. Consistent practice helps reinforce the habit.

Combine with Other Routines:
- Pair meditation with other daily routines, such as after your morning coffee, before starting work, or after exercising.

Track Your Progress:
- Keep a meditation journal to note your experiences, any challenges, and the benefits you observe over time. This can motivate you to continue and deepen your practice.

Join a Community:

- Consider joining a meditation group or online community for support, accountability, and shared experiences.

By integrating meditation into your daily life, you can enhance your career performance, improve your well-being, and create a foundation for lasting success and fulfillment.

NOTES

Daily Meditation Practice

Morning Meditation Routine

Starting your day with meditation can set a positive tone and help you approach your tasks with clarity and calm. Here's a step-by-step guide to an effective morning meditation routine:

Wake Up and Hydrate:
- Begin by drinking a glass of water to hydrate your body and mind. This helps you feel more alert and ready for meditation.

Find a Comfortable Space:
- Choose a quiet, comfortable spot where you won't be disturbed. It could be a dedicated meditation area, a corner of your bedroom, or a cozy chair.

Set Your Intention:
- Take a moment to set an intention for your meditation. This could be to cultivate focus, reduce stress, or start the day with gratitude.

Practice Deep Breathing:
- Sit comfortably with your back straight and close your eyes. Take a few deep breaths, inhaling through your nose and exhaling through your mouth. Focus on the sensation of your breath.

Mindfulness Meditation:
- Spend 5-10 minutes observing your breath. Notice the rise and fall of your chest or the sensation of air passing through your nostrils. If your mind wanders, gently bring your focus back to your breath.

Visualization:
- Visualize your day ahead. Imagine yourself moving through your tasks with ease and confidence. See yourself handling challenges calmly and successfully achieving your goals.

Express Gratitude:

- Conclude your meditation by thinking of three things you are grateful for. This can help shift your mindset to a positive, appreciative state.

Stretch and Transition:
- After meditating, take a few moments to stretch and gently transition into your day. This helps integrate the calm and focus you've cultivated into your morning routine.

NOTES

Midday Mindfulness

Taking a mindfulness break during the day can refresh your mind and improve your productivity. Here's how to incorporate a midday mindfulness practice:

- **Schedule a Break**:
    - Set a reminder to take a 5-10 minute break during your workday. Ideally, schedule it during a time when you feel your energy dipping or need a mental reset.
- **Find a Quiet Spot**:
    - Step away from your workspace and find a quiet place where you can sit comfortably. If you can't leave your desk, simply close your eyes and sit upright.
- **Practice Deep Breathing**:

- Close your eyes and take several deep breaths. Inhale slowly through your nose, hold for a few seconds, and exhale through your mouth. Focus on the rhythm of your breath.

Body Scan:

- Perform a quick body scan to release tension. Starting from your head, mentally scan down to your toes, noticing any areas of tightness or discomfort. Breathe into those areas and consciously relax them.

Mindful Observation:

- Open your eyes and spend a few minutes mindfully observing your surroundings. Notice the details, colors, and textures around you. This helps anchor you in the present moment and provides a mental reset.

Positive Affirmations:

- Repeat a few positive affirmations to boost your mood and motivation. For example, "I am capable and focused," or "I handle challenges with grace and ease."

Transition Back to Work:

- After your mindfulness break, take a moment to stretch and refocus before returning to your tasks. Notice how this short practice has refreshed your mind and body

NOTES

Evening Relaxation

An evening meditation routine can help you unwind from the day and prepare for restful sleep. Here's a step-by-step guide:

Create a Calming Environment:
- Choose a quiet, comfortable spot and dim the lights. Consider playing soft, calming music or using a white noise machine to create a relaxing atmosphere.

Unplug and Disconnect:
- Turn off electronic devices or put them on silent mode. Allow yourself to disconnect from work and external distractions.

Practice Deep Breathing:
- Sit or lie down comfortably and close your eyes. Take slow, deep breaths, inhaling through your nose and exhaling through your mouth. Focus on the sensation of your breath.

Progressive Muscle Relaxation:
- Starting from your feet, gradually tense and then relax each muscle group in your

body. Move upwards, ending with your face and head. This helps release physical tension.

Guided Meditation:
- Listen to a guided meditation designed for relaxation and sleep. You can find many options online or through meditation apps. Follow the guidance to help your mind and body unwind.

Reflect on Your Day:
- Spend a few minutes reflecting on your day. Acknowledge your accomplishments and any challenges you faced. Let go of any lingering stress or worries.

Visualize a Peaceful Place:
- Imagine a serene place where you feel completely relaxed and at peace. It could be a beach, forest, or any place that brings you comfort. Visualize yourself in this place, absorbing the calm and tranquility.

Gratitude Practice:
- Conclude your meditation by thinking of three things you are grateful for from the day. This can help shift your focus to

positive experiences and promote a sense of contentment.

Prepare for Sleep:
- After your meditation, maintain a calm and quiet environment. Avoid engaging in stimulating activities and allow yourself to drift into a restful sleep.

By incorporating these daily meditation practices into your routine, you can enhance your mental clarity, reduce stress, and improve your overall well-being, ultimately supporting your career growth and personal development

NOTES

Deepening Your Meditation Practice

Advanced Meditation Techniques

As you become more comfortable with basic meditation practices, you may want to explore advanced techniques to deepen your experience. Here are some methods to enhance your meditation:

Loving-Kindness Meditation (Metta)
- **Purpose**: Cultivates compassion and empathy towards yourself and others.
- **How to Practice**:

Sit comfortably and close your eyes.
Begin by focusing on yourself.
Silently repeat phrases like
"May I be happy.
May I be healthy.
May I be safe.
May I live with ease."
Gradually extend these wishes to others: first to loved ones, then to
neutral people, and finally to those with whom you have difficulties.
Visualize each person as you repeat the phrases, and sincerely wish them well.

Body Scan Meditation
- **Purpose**: Enhances body awareness and promotes relaxation.
- **How to Practice**:
    Lie down or sit comfortably and close your eyes.
    Bring your attention to your feet, noticing any sensations.
    Slowly move your attention up your body, part by part, all the way to the top of your head.
    Take your time with each area, observing sensations without judgment.

If you notice tension, breathe into that area and imagine it relaxing.

Chakra Meditation

- **Purpose**: Balances and aligns the body's energy centers (chakras).
- **How to Practice**:
    - Sit comfortably and close your eyes.
    - Focus on each chakra, starting from the base of your spine to the crown of your head.
    - Visualize each chakra as a spinning wheel of energy, using its associated color (e.g., red for the root chakra, orange for the sacral chakra).
    - Imagine energy flowing freely through each chakra, removing any blockages.

Breathwork (Pranayama)

- **Purpose**: Enhances control over breath, calming the mind and energizing the body.
- **How to Practice**:
    - **Nadi Shodhana (Alternate Nostril Breathing)**:
        - Close your right nostril with your thumb, inhale through your left

Nostril. Close your left nostril with your ring finger, exhale through your
right nostril.
Inhale through your right nostril, close it, and exhale through your
left nostril.
Repeat for several cycles.

Kapalabhati (Skull Shining Breath):
Take a deep breath in, then exhale forcefully through your nose
while pulling your belly towards your spine.
Allow the inhalation to happen passively. Perform this in quick
succession.
Start with 20 breaths and gradually increase the count.

NOTES

Creating a Deep Meditation Practice

To deepen your meditation practice, consider incorporating the following tips into your routine:

Regularity and Consistency
- Set a regular meditation schedule and stick to it. Aim to meditate at the same time each day to build a habit.
- Start with shorter sessions and gradually increase the duration as you become more comfortable.

Setting a Peaceful Environment
- Create a dedicated meditation space that is quiet, comfortable, and free from distractions.
- Use props like cushions, mats, or blankets to enhance your comfort.
- Consider adding elements like candles, incense, or calming music to create a serene atmosphere.

Mindfulness in Daily Activities
- Incorporate mindfulness into your everyday activities. Practice being fully present while eating, walking, or working.
- Focus on the sensations, thoughts, and feelings that arise in each moment.

Journaling Your Experiences

- Keep a meditation journal to track your experiences, insights, and any challenges you encounter.
- Reflecting on your practice can help you identify patterns, areas for improvement, and the benefits you're experiencing.

Seek Guidance and Community
- Join a meditation group or community to share experiences, gain support, and learn from others.
- Consider attending meditation retreats or workshops to deepen your practice under the guidance of experienced teachers.

Patience and Self-Compassion
- Remember that meditation is a journey, and progress may be slow. Be patient with yourself and recognize that every meditation session is beneficial, even if it doesn't feel perfect.
- Treat yourself with kindness and compassion, acknowledging that it's normal to experience challenges and distractions.

NOTES

Overcoming Common Challenges

Even experienced meditators face challenges. Here are some common issues and how to overcome them:

Restlessness and Distraction
- Acknowledge distractions without judgment and gently bring your focus back to your breath or chosen point of focus.
- Try shorter sessions if you find it difficult to stay still, gradually increasing the duration as your practice deepens.

Sleepiness
- If you feel drowsy during meditation, try practicing at a different time of day when you're more alert.
- Sit up straight instead of lying down, and ensure your meditation space is well-lit.

Impatience and Frustration
- Recognize that impatience is a common experience and part of the learning process.
- Remind yourself of the benefits of meditation and the long-term goals you're working towards.

Physical Discomfort
- Use props like cushions or chairs to support a comfortable posture.

- Practice gentle stretching or yoga before meditation to relieve tension in your body.

By incorporating these advanced techniques, tips, and strategies, you can deepen your meditation practice, enhance your mindfulness, and experience greater benefits in both your personal and professional life.

NOTES

The Power of Manifestation

Understanding Manifestation

Manifestation is the process of bringing your desires and goals into reality through focused thought, intention, and action. It involves aligning your mindset, emotions, and behaviors with what you want to achieve. Here's how to understand and practice manifestation effectively:

The Law of Attraction
- o The law of attraction states that like attracts like. Positive thoughts and feelings attract positive outcomes, while negative thoughts and feelings attract negative outcomes.
- o By maintaining a positive mindset and focusing on your goals, you can attract the

circumstances and opportunities needed to achieve them.

The Power of Intention

- Setting a clear intention is the first step in manifesting your desires. Your intention should be specific, positive, and focused on what you want to achieve.

- Example: Instead of saying, "I don't want to be stressed at work," say, "I intend to remain calm and focused in all my tasks."

NOTES

Steps to Manifest Your Desires

Clarify Your Goals

- o Take time to clearly define what you want to manifest. Be specific about your goals and ensure they align with your true desires.
- o Example: If your goal is career advancement, specify the role you want, the skills you need, and the steps required to get there.

Visualize Your Success

- o Visualization involves creating a mental image of yourself achieving your goals. This helps reinforce your intentions and makes your goals feel more tangible.

- Spend a few minutes each day visualizing your success. Imagine the details, emotions, and outcomes associated with achieving your desires.

Practice Positive Affirmations
- Affirmations are positive statements that help reprogram your subconscious mind to support your goals
- Create affirmations that reflect your desires and repeat them daily. Ensure they are in the present tense and reflect a positive outcome.
- Example: "I am confident and successful in my career."

Cultivate a Positive Mindset
- Focus on maintaining a positive attitude and outlook. This involves being mindful of your thoughts, words, and actions.
- Practice gratitude to reinforce positive thinking. Regularly acknowledge and appreciate the good things in your life.

Take Inspired Action
- Manifestation is not just about thinking and visualizing; it also requires taking action towards your goals.
- Identify actionable steps you can take to move closer to your desires. Break down your goals into manageable tasks and commit to working on them regularly.

- Example: If you want to learn a new skill, enroll in a course, set aside time for practice, and seek feedback to improve.

Overcome Limiting Beliefs

- Limiting beliefs are negative thoughts and attitudes that hold you back from achieving your goals. Identify and challenge these beliefs.
- Replace limiting beliefs with empowering ones. For example, change "I'm not good enough" to "I am capable and deserving of success."

Stay Patient and Persistent

- Manifestation takes time, and it's important to remain patient and persistent. Trust the process and stay committed to your goals.
- Regularly review your progress and adjust your actions as needed. Celebrate small victories and keep moving forward.

NOTES

Manifestation Techniques

Vision Boards
- Create a vision board by collecting images, quotes, and symbols that represent your goals. Display it where you can see it daily to keep your desires top of mind.

Scripting
- Write a detailed narrative of your life as if you have already achieved your goals. Describe how you feel, what you do, and the impact on your life. Read it regularly to reinforce your intentions.

Meditation and Mindfulness
- Incorporate meditation and mindfulness practices to enhance your focus and clarity. Use meditation to visualize your goals and affirm your intentions.

Gratitude Journaling
- Keep a gratitude journal to regularly acknowledge and appreciate the positive aspects of your life. This helps maintain a positive mindset and attracts more good into your life.

NOTES

Example Manifestation Practices

Morning Manifestation Routine
- Start your day with a few minutes of visualization and positive affirmations. Set clear intentions for the day and focus on taking steps towards your goals.

Evening Reflection
- Spend a few minutes before bed reflecting on your day. Acknowledge your progress, express gratitude, and reaffirm your goals.

Regular Check-ins
- Schedule regular check-ins to review your goals, adjust your actions, and reinforce your intentions. This helps keep you on track and motivated.

By understanding and practicing these manifestation techniques, you can align your thoughts, emotions, and actions with your desires, ultimately bringing your goals into reality.

NOTES

Steps to Manifesting Your Career Goals

Clarify Your Career Goals

Identify Your Desires
- Take time to reflect on what you truly want in your career. Consider your passions, interests, and values. Ask yourself what makes you feel fulfilled and motivated.

Set Specific Goals
- Define clear and specific career goals. Instead of a vague goal like "I want to be successful," specify what success looks like for you. Example: "I want to become a senior marketing manager at a leading tech company within the next three years."

Write Down Your Goals
- Writing down your goals makes them more tangible and real. It also serves as a constant reminder of what you are working towards.

NOTES

Visualize Your Success

Create a Mental Image
- o Spend a few minutes each day visualizing yourself achieving your career goals. Imagine the details of your success: your workplace, your role, your interactions

with colleagues, and your accomplishments.

Use All Senses
- Make your visualization as vivid as possible by engaging all your senses. Feel the emotions of success, hear the sounds of your work environment, and see the specific details of your surroundings.

Maintain a Vision Board
- Create a vision board with images, quotes, and symbols that represent your career goals. Display it where you can see it daily to reinforce your vision.

NOTES

Practice Positive Affirmations

Create Affirmations
- Develop positive affirmations that align with your career goals. Example: "I am a confident and skilled professional, attracting opportunities for growth and success."

Repeat Daily
- Repeat your affirmations daily, preferably in the morning and before bed. Consistent repetition helps reprogram your subconscious mind to support your goals.

Believe in Your Affirmations

- Say your affirmations with conviction and belief. Feel the truth and power behind your words.

NOTES

Cultivate a Positive Mindset

Focus on Positivity
- Maintain a positive outlook by focusing on what's going well in your career and life. Practice gratitude to reinforce positive thinking.

Surround Yourself with Positivity
- Engage with positive and supportive people who uplift and inspire you. Avoid negative influences that drain your energy and motivation.

Reframe Challenges
- View challenges as opportunities for growth and learning. Approach problems with a solution-oriented mindset.

NOTES

Take Inspired Action

Break Down Goals
- Divide your career goals into smaller, actionable steps. Create a plan with specific tasks and deadlines to stay on track.

Stay Consistent
- Consistently work towards your goals, even if progress seems slow. Small, regular actions accumulate to create significant results over time.

Seek Opportunities
- Be proactive in seeking opportunities for growth and advancement. Network, attend workshops, and volunteer for projects that align with your goals.

NOTES

Overcome Limiting Beliefs

Identify Limiting Beliefs
- Recognize any negative beliefs or thoughts that hinder your progress. Common limiting beliefs include "I'm not good enough" or "I don't have the skills."

Challenge and Replace
- Challenge these beliefs by questioning their validity. Replace them with empowering beliefs. Example: Change "I'm not experienced enough" to "I am continually gaining valuable experience and skills."

Seek Support
- Consider working with a coach or mentor to help identify and overcome limiting beliefs. Surround yourself with people who believe in your potential.

NOTES

Stay Patient and Persistent

Trust the Process
- Understand that manifestation takes time. Trust the process and stay committed to your goals, even when progress seems slow.

Stay Resilient
- Maintain resilience in the face of setbacks. Learn from failures and use them as stepping stones towards success.

Celebrate Milestones
- Celebrate your achievements, no matter how small. Acknowledging your progress boosts motivation and reinforces positive behavior.

NOTES

_____
_____
_____
_____
_____
_____
_____
_____
_____
_____
_____
_____
_____
_____
_____
_____
_____
_____
_____
_____

Example Practice for Manifesting Career Goals

Morning Routine
- Start your day with visualization and affirmations. Set intentions for the day that align with your career goals.

Journaling

- Keep a journal to track your progress, reflect on your experiences, and write about your goals and aspirations.

Evening Reflection
- Spend a few minutes before bed reviewing your day. Reflect on your achievements, express gratitude, and reaffirm your goals.

By following these steps, you can effectively manifest your career goals. Remember, manifestation is a continuous process that combines mindset, intention, and action. Stay focused, positive, and proactive, and you will gradually see your career goals come to fruition.

NOTES

Maintaining Your Progress

Consistency is Key

Weekly Check-Ins

- **Set Aside Time**: Dedicate 15-30 minutes each week to review your progress. Use this time to reflect on your achievements, challenges, and lessons learned.
- **Questions to Ask**: Consider questions such as:

- What went well this week?
- What challenges did I face and how did I overcome them?
- What can I improve for next week?

Monthly Reviews
- **Assess Your Goals**: At the end of each month, evaluate your progress towards your larger career goals. Adjust your strategies and set new targets if necessary.
- **Celebrate Milestones**: Recognize and celebrate your accomplishments. This boosts motivation and reinforces positive behavior.
- **Review the Year**: Reflect on your overall progress and growth throughout the year. Identify key achievements, significant challenges, and areas for improvement.
- **Set New Goals**: Based on your reflections, set new career goals for the upcoming year. Create a plan to achieve them with actionable steps.

NOTES

Staying Flexible and Adaptable

Embrace Change
- **Be Open to New Opportunities**: Stay open to unexpected opportunities and changes in your career path. Flexibility allows you to adapt and thrive in different circumstances.
- **Reevaluate Goals**: Periodically reassess your career goals to ensure they align with your current values, interests, and circumstances.

Develop a Growth Mindset
- **Embrace Challenges**: View challenges as opportunities to learn and grow. Approach problems with a solution-oriented mindset.
- **Learn Continuously**: Commit to lifelong learning and self-improvement. Seek out new skills, knowledge, and experiences that enhance your career.

NOTES

Seeking Feedback and Support

Request Constructive Feedback
- **From Colleagues and Supervisors**: Regularly ask for feedback on your performance from colleagues and supervisors. Constructive feedback helps you identify strengths and areas for improvement.

- **Use Feedback Effectively**: Analyze the feedback and create an action plan to address any areas needing improvement. Use positive feedback to reinforce successful behaviors.

Build a Support Network
- **Mentors and Coaches**: Seek guidance from mentors and career coaches who can provide valuable insights, advice, and support.
- **Professional Communities**: Join professional associations, networking groups, and online communities related to your field. Engaging with like-minded individuals can offer support, inspiration, and opportunities.

NOTES

Balancing Work and Personal Life

Prioritize Self-Care
- **Physical Health**: Maintain a healthy lifestyle through regular exercise, balanced nutrition, and sufficient sleep. Good physical health supports mental clarity and productivity.
- **Mental Health**: Practice stress-management techniques such as mindfulness, meditation, and hobbies that relax and rejuvenate you.

Set Boundaries
- **Work-Life Balance**: Establish clear boundaries between work and personal life. Ensure you allocate time for relaxation, family, and personal interests.
- **Time Management**: Use time management techniques like the Pomodoro Technique or time blocking to increase productivity and ensure you have time for both work and personal activities.

Mindful Breaks
- **Scheduled Breaks**: Take regular breaks during your workday to recharge. Short breaks can improve focus and prevent burnout.
- **Mindfulness Practices**: Use breaks to practice mindfulness or light physical activity. This helps reset your mind and body, enhancing overall well-being.

NOTES

Tracking and Adjusting Your Action Plan

Use Tracking Tools
- o **Task Management Apps**: Utilize apps like Todoist, Trello, or Asana to organize and track your tasks and goals. Regularly update these tools to reflect your progress.
- o **Progress Logs**: Keep a log of your daily or weekly activities related to your career

goals. This helps you stay accountable and recognize patterns in your efforts.

Adjust Your Plan as Needed
- **Be Flexible**: Recognize when certain strategies or actions are not working. Be willing to adjust your plan and try new approaches to achieve your goals.
- **Set Realistic Milestones**: Break down your larger goals into smaller, manageable milestones. Adjust these milestones as needed based on your progress and any changes in your circumstances.

NOTES

Staying Motivated

Revisit Your Vision Board
- **Daily Reminders**: Keep your vision board in a place where you see it daily. Regularly reviewing it helps keep your goals and aspirations top of mind.
- **Update as Needed**: Refresh your vision board periodically to reflect any new goals or changes in your aspirations.

Celebrate Small Wins
- **Recognize Progress**: Celebrate small achievements and milestones along the way. Acknowledging progress keeps you

motivated and reinforces positive behavior.
- **Reward Yourself**: Treat yourself to small rewards for meeting goals or completing significant tasks. This adds an element of fun and motivation to your journey.

By maintaining your progress with these strategies, you can ensure steady advancement towards your career goals. Regular review, adaptability, support, balance, tracking, and motivation are key components in sustaining your journey towards success.

NOTES

Embracing Your Journey

Congratulations on completing this guide! You've taken a significant step towards manifesting your career goals and creating a fulfilling professional life. Remember, the journey to success is a continuous process of growth, learning, and adaptation. Your career journey is unique, and you have the power to shape it according to your dreams and aspirations. By leveraging the practices and tools outlined in this guide, you can create a fulfilling and successful professional life. Remember, you are capable of achieving greatness, and every step you take brings you closer to your goals. Believe in yourself, stay committed, and embrace the journey with an open heart and mind. Your career success is within reach, and you have the tools and strategies to manifest it. Here's to your continued growth, achievement, and fulfillment. Go forth and manifest the career of your dreams!

Thank you for choosing this guide to accompany you on your career journey. We wish you all the success and happiness in your professional endeavors. Keep striving, keep believing, and keep manifesting your dreams into reality.

Luchrisha Harrison

NOTES

www.ingramcontent.com/pod-product-compliance
Lightning Source LLC
Chambersburg PA
CBHW071834210526
45479CB00001B/134